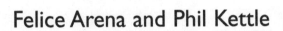

BO...

Felice Arena and Phil Kettle

illustrated by
gus Gordon

RISING ★ STARS

5143533

...at Britain by
...TD 2005
...romley, BR1 4BH
...ice)

For information visit our website at:
www.risingstars-uk.com

British Library Cataloguing in Publication Data

A CIP record for this book is available from the British Library.

ISBN: 1-905056-14-1

First published in 2004 by
MACMILLAN EDUCATION AUSTRALIA PTY LTD
627 Chapel Street, South Yarra, Australia 3141

Visit our website at www.macmillan.com.au

Associated companies and representatives throughout the world.

Copyright © Felice Arena and Phil Kettle 2004

Project Management by Limelight Press Pty Ltd
Cover and text design by Lore Foye
Illustrations by Gus Gordon

Printed and bound in Great Britain by
Mackays of Chatham plc, Chatham, Kent

BOYS RULE!

Contents

Sam

Billy

CHAPTER 1

Rain Games

Best friends Billy and Sam are hanging out together one rainy Saturday at Billy's house.

Billy "I wish the rain would stop. Then we could ride our bikes."

Sam "Yes. It's really coming down. You sure your mum won't let us play outside?"

Billy "No. I've already asked a million times. She said we should be able to entertain ourselves *indoors*."

Sam "So, what are we going to do?"

Billy "Want to watch TV? Or a DVD?"

Sam "No. I've seen all the movies you've got."

Billy "No you haven't. What about 'Killer Bunnies'?"

Sam "Seen it!"

Billy "You sure? The one where a bunch of rabbits grow really long fangs and take over a small town."

Sam "And they're as tall as the humans—yes, I've seen it."

Billy "Okay then, want to play a game? I've got a new computer game called 'Super Hero Racing'."

Sam "Cool!"

Billy and Sam sit in front of Billy's computer. Billy explains the rules of the game to Sam while it's loading.

Billy "You've got ten superheroes to pick from. Once you choose the hero you're going to be, you have to race each other around the world. You have to jump over mountains and bust through buildings. You can fly, run or swim. The first one back to the starting place is the winner. I'm going to be Super Bull Man ... half-man, half-bull."

Sam "I'll be Super Stallican …
half-stallion, half-pelican."
Billy "Okay. Ready, go!"

Billy and Sam frantically click and
move their joysticks. It's a close race
but Billy makes it over the finishing
line first.

Billy "Yes! In your face! I'm the winner! Champion of the world! And you're the loser! Woo-hoo!"

Billy begins to do a funny dance in front of Sam.

Sam "What are you doing?"

Billy "It's my victory dance. Yeah! I'm the greatest! And you're not!"

Sam "It's only one game. And now that I know what to do, I challenge you to a re-match. And this time I'll beat you!"

Billy "Okay, you're on!"

CHAPTER 2

Show Me the Money

Billy and Sam play another game of "Super Hero Racing". Again, Billy is the winner and again he rubs it in Sam's face. Sam wants to keep playing until he wins. Twenty times later he still hasn't beaten his friend.

Sam "I hate this game."

Billy "You're just saying that
because you can't beat me. Ha, ha!"

Sam "Well, let's play something else.
Then you'll see who's laughing."

Billy "Okay! But I've got to tell you
I'm the king of all games!
Computer games, board games,
whatever. You won't be able to
beat me at any of them."

Sam "Yeah, right. Just you wait and see ... king of big heads!"

Billy "Okay, forget the computer. How about Monopoly?"

Sam "Now you're talking, dude!"

Billy and Sam set up the Monopoly board on the kitchen table. Billy decides to be "banker" and deals out some money to himself and Sam. The boys choose their counters.

Billy "I want the dog!"

Sam "I'll be the car!"

Billy "Right, we have to throw the dice. Whoever gets the highest number starts. Here goes ... 6! Yes!"

Sam rolls the dice. It shows a 2.

Billy "And the champ of the world makes his move!"

Billy rolls the dice and it shows a 5. He moves his counter.

Billy "One, two, three, four, five! Kings Cross Station. Yep, I'm going to buy it. Your turn."

Sam rolls the dice. It also shows a 5. He moves his marker onto Kings Cross Station.

Billy "Aha! That's mine! Hand over the cash, boy!"

The boys continue to play Monopoly for over an hour. Eventually Billy wins. This time he does his victory dance on top of the kitchen table.

Sam "Stop dancing, will you? I challenge you to another game. Got any playing cards? I'll show you!"

CHAPTER 3

Snap!

Billy gets out a pack of cards and shuffles them. He divides them into two halves and hands one half of the cards to Sam.

Billy "Right, do you know how to play Snap?"

Sam "Umm, derr! Of course I do. Now *this* game I know I can beat you at!"

Billy "Yes, keep dreaming! 'Cos remember I'm the king of ... "

Sam "Yes, yes, the king of all games. I got it. But not this one! Let's play!"

Billy and Sam place their cards on the table, one on top of the other, watching for their chance to win.

Billy "Snap!"
Billy "Snap!"
Sam "Snap!"
Billy "Snap!"
Billy "Snap!"

Sam begins to feel frustrated as it looks like Billy is going to win again. Sam imagines Billy is a fly and he is about to swat him with his giant hand.

Sam "Snap!"

Billy "That's not a pair! Where's your head? What are you thinking?"

Sam "Nothing. Just daydreaming."

Billy "Well, I wouldn't daydream if I were you. That's no way to beat a world champion like myself. Snap!"

A few minutes later the game is over. Sam has lost ... again. Billy suddenly does a handstand.

Sam "Now what are you doing?"

Billy "Well, I got bored with my
victory dance. So this is my victory
handstand. I am the *greatest*! And
you're not!"

Sam (whispering to himself) "What
a show-off! I have to beat him at
something. But what? ... I know!"

CHAPTER 4

Noble Knight

Sam suggests that he and Billy try their hand at chess.

Billy (chuckling) "Chess?"

Sam "What? You chicken? Scared that I'm actually going to beat you this time?"

Billy "Huh! Yeah, right! I'm the king of chess too, you know! So, are you sure you want to lose another game?"

Sam "There's no way I'm going to lose this one. Chess is a thinking person's game. You need brains to play."

Billy (snorting) "Huh! Then dude, you're going to get whupped again!"

Billy runs up to his bedroom and returns a few moments later with a chessboard and its pieces.

Billy "Right, I'll move my knight here."

Sam "Then I'll move my knight and take your bishop, thanks very much!"

Billy "That was dumb, 'cos now I can take your queen."

Sam starts to daydream again. He imagines that he and Billy are noble knights on their horses about to charge at each other.

Billy "Come on! Stop daydreaming. Your move."

Sam "Aha! Gotcha! My king strikes and takes your poor old queen."

Billy "Yes!"

Sam "What? What did I do?"

CHAPTER 5

Just One More

Sam worriedly looks down at the chessboard while Billy is grinning from ear to ear.

Billy "You just blew it! Checkmate!"

Sam "What? No way! How?"

Billy "See my knight. And there it goes. Say goodbye to your king!"

Billy jumps to his feet and breaks out into his victory dance. Sam drops his head into his hands.

Billy "Hey, it's okay. You can't expect to be good at everything. You just can't beat me at games. I told you I was the king."

Sam "But even kings can lose their crowns, you know."

Billy "Yes, but not me. Hey, still friends?"

Sam "I suppose so. But if you were a real friend you'd let me choose one more game."

Billy "Sam, you don't want to ... "

Sam "Come on, just one more!"

Billy "Fine! But don't cry like a baby when I crush you again. What game do you want to play?"

Sam "What about Stone, Paper, Scissors?"

Billy "Sure!"

Sam "And if I win, then will you forget all the games you've won today and crown me the king of all games?"

Billy "Yes, okay."

Sam "What? Really?"

Billy "Yep, really, because you're going to lose again anyway."

Sam and Billy clench their fists, ready to make the action for stone, paper or scissors.

Billy "Wait up. Paper beats stone because you can wrap it over it, right?"

Sam "Yep."

Billy "And scissors beats paper because they can cut through it. But scissors can't beat stone because they can't cut through it. Right?"

Sam "Yep. That's it. I thought you said you were king of all games."

Billy "I am, and don't you forget it. So, bring it on. I can feel another dance coming!"

Sam and Billy shake their fists.

Billy and Sam "One, two, three!"

Sam makes the action for paper while Billy makes a stone shape.

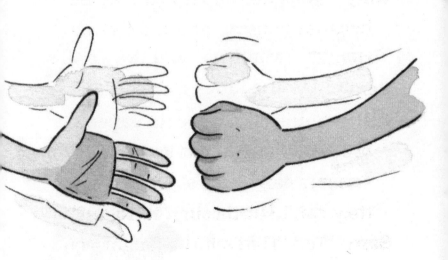

Sam "I've won! I've won! I've finally won! I'm the king of all games!"

Sam suddenly dances around Billy.

Sam "Hey, this is the coolest victory dance ever! I just wanted to save the best till last!"

BOYS RULE!

Games Lingo

Billy

Sam

dice Small cubes with a different number of dots on each side, from 1 up to 6.

friend The perfect person to play a game with!

game An activity that is entertaining and fun.

joystick A control device on a computer or video game that guides you on screen.

Monopoly A board game where you can buy houses and hotels with fake money.

victory When you have beaten your opponent.

BOYS RULE!

Games Must-dos

☞ Try to keep all your board games in one spot so that you know where to find them when you next want to play with them.

☞ Be gracious when you win. No-one likes a show-off.

☞ Don't go too crazy with a joystick— it could break.

☞ Find a large flat surface area to play your games on, such as a kitchen table or the floor.

☞ Have plenty of snacks and drinks nearby … to help you play better. It's tiring stuff, competing!

☞ Make up your own games. Use pencils and paper to design your own board game and decide on some rules of play.

☞ Always have fun. Remember … it's only a game!

☞ Games that don't need any equipment to play them can often be the best fun, especially on long car trips. Invent some memory games and remember to remember the rules!

☞ Have your own Battle of the Games with some friends, but you have to make up your own victory dance if you win!

BOYS RULE!

Games
Instant Info

The most expensive Monopoly set in the world is worth 2 million pounds. It's made out of gold, rubies, sapphires and diamonds.

One of the greatest chess players in the world is Gary Kasparov from Russia.

PlayStation 2 is a video game system that not only has cool games but is also able to play DVDs and CDs. Tell your parents that it is cheap at half the price!

Five fun board games to play are Scrabble, Monopoly, Draughts, Backgammon and Cluedo.

The English board game Cluedo is called Clue in America.

Bingo is played around the world by a lot of people.

Snap is the name of a (really easy) card game.

Snakes and Ladders, based on an early Indian game called Moksha-Patamu, was first played by the Victorians in 1892.

One of the most popular Nintendo games is "Super Mario Brothers".

BOYS RULE!

Think Tank

1 Snap is a card game. True or False?

2 Is there a "prince" piece in the game of chess?

3 What's the highest number you can throw with a pair of dice?

4 What's the one thing you try to have when playing a game?

5 What sort of stick do you often use to play computer games, especially ones that require speed or direction?

6 What sort of weather is great for playing indoor games?

7 Is there such a device as a Game Girl?

8 Have you ever won a game?

Answers

How did you score?

- If you got all 8 answers correct, then you definitely love to play games and have the right to call yourself the king of all games!

- If you got 6 answers correct, you're also a great game player but probably need to brush up on the rules sometimes.

- If you got fewer than 4 answers correct, then games don't seem to interest you much. But you'll always be around to join in if your friends want you to play.

Felice → ← Phil

Hi Guys!

We have heaps of fun reading and want you to, too. We both believe that being a good reader is really important and so cool.

Try out our suggestions to help you have fun as you read.

At school, why don't you use "Battle of the Games" as a play and you and your friends can be the actors. Set the scene for your play. Bring some games to school to use as props but leave your computers at home! And make sure the desk you use for the victory dance is strong enough.

So ... have you decided who is going to be Billy and who is going to be Sam? Now, with your friends, read and act out our story in front of the class.

We have a lot of fun when we go to schools and read our stories. After we finish the kids all clap really loudly. When you've finished your play your classmates will do the same. Just remember to look out the window—there might be a talent scout from a television station watching you!

Reading at home is really important and a lot of fun as well.

Take our books home and get someone in your family to read them with you. Maybe they can take on a part in the story.

Remember, reading is a whole lot of fun.

So, as the frog in the local pond would say, Read-it!

And remember, Boys Rule!

Felice

BOYS RULE!
When We Were Kids

Phil

Phil "I used to love playing Snakes and Ladders!"

Felice "Oh, yeah. I remember that game. I always had trouble keeping the snakes in one spot. They'd always slither away."

Phil "What? You used real snakes?"

Felice "Yeah. Well, how else do you play Snakes and Ladders?"

Phil "It's a board game, silly! You're not supposed to play with real snakes!"

Felice "Oh! That explains why I was never good at it!"

BOYS RULE!

What a Laugh!

Q What did the mini Scrabble set say to the mini Monopoly set?

A I'm a little bored.

BOYS RULE!

Gone Fishing

The Tree House

Golf Legends

Camping Out

Bike Daredevils

Water Rats

Skateboard Dudes

Tennis Ace

Basketball Buddies

Secret Agent Heroes

Wet World

Rock Star

Pirate Attack

Olympic Champions

Race Car Dreamers

Hit the Beach

Rotten School Day

Halloween Gotcha!

Battle of the Games

On the Farm